RANADE
GANDHI & JINNAH

RANADE
GANDHI & JINNAH

ADDRESS DELIVERED
ON THE 101ST BIRTHDAY CELEBRATION OF
MAHADEV GOVIND RANADE
HELD ON THE 18TH JANUARY 1943
IN THE GOKHALE MEMORIAL HALL, POONA

By
The Hon'ble Dr. B. R. AMBEDKAR
M.A., Ph.D., D.Sc., BARRISTER-AT-LAW
Member, Governor-General's Executive Council

GYAN

ISBN : 978-81-212-9052-4 (HB)

First Publication in 1943

Published by

GYAN

Gyan Publishing House
5, Ansari Road
Daryaganj, New Delhi-110002
Phone: 9811692060
E-mail: books@gyanbooks.com

Printed at: G. Print Process, Delhi.

Contents

Preface

The Deccan Sabha of Poona invited me to deliver an address on the 101st birthday of the late Justice Mahadev Govind Ranade which it proposed to celebrate and which fell on the 18th January 1940. I was not very willing to accept the invitation. For I knew that my views on social and political problems, a discussion of which could not be avoided in a discourse on Ranade, would not very pleasing to the audience and even perhaps to the members of the Deccan Sabha. In the end I accepted their invitation. At the time when I delivered the Address I had no intention of publishing it. Addresses delivered on anniversaries of Great Men are generally occasional pieces. They do not have much permanent value. I did not think that my address was an exception to this. But I have some troublesome friends who have been keen on seeing the whole of it in print and have been insisting upon it. I am indifferent to the idea. I am quite content with the publicity it has receiver and I have no desire to seek more. At the same time if there are people who think that it is worthy of being rescued from falling into oblivion, I do not see any reason for disappointing them.

The address as printed differs from the address as delivered in two respects. Section X of the address was omitted from the address as delivered to prevent the performance going beyond [a] reasonable time. Even without it, it took one hour and a half to deliver the address. This is one difference. The other difference lies in the omission of a large portion of Section VIII which was devoted to a comparison of Ranade with Phule. For this omission there are two reasons. In the first place, the comparison was not sufficiently full and detailed to do justice to the two men; in the second place, when the difficulties of finding enough paper compelled me to sacrifice some portion of the address, this appeared to be best offering.

The publication of the address is taking place under peculiar circumstances. Ordinarily reviews follow publication. In this case the situation is reversed. What is worse is that the reviews have condemned the address in scathing terms. This is a matter primarily for the publishers to worry about. I am happy that the publisher knows the risk and he takes it. Nothing more need be said about it except that it supports the view taken by my friends that the address contains matter which is of more than ephemeral value. As for myself I am not in the least perturbed by the condemnation of this address by the Press. What is the ground for its condemnation? And who has come forward to condemn it?

I am condemned because I criticized Mr. Gandhi and Mr. Jinnah for the mess they have made of Indian politics, and that in doing so I am alleged to have shown towards them hatred and disrespect. In reply to this charge what I have to say is that I have been a critic and I must continue to be such. It may be I am making mistakes, but I have always felt that it is better to make mistakes than to accept guidance and direction from others or to sit silent and allow things to deteriorate. Those who have accused me of having been actuated by feelings of hatred forget two things. In the first place this alleged hatred is not born of anything that can be called personal. If I am against them, it is because I want a settlement. I want a settlement of some sort, and I am not prepared to wait for an ideal settlement. Nor can I tolerate [for] anyone on whose will and consent settlement depends, to stand on [his] dignity and play the Grand Moghul. In the second place, no one can hope to make any effective mark upon his time, and bring the aid that is worth bringing to great principles and struggling causes, if he is not strong in his love and his hatred. I hate injustice, tyranny, pompousness and humbug, and my hatred embraces all those who are guilty of them. I want to tell my critics that I regard my feelings of hatred as a real force. They are only the reflex of the love I bear for the causes I believe in, and I am in no wise ashamed of it. For these reasons I tender no apology for my criticism of Mr. Gandhi and Mr. Jinnah, the two men who have brought India's political progress to a standstill.

The condemnation is by the Congress Press. I know the Congress Press well. I attach no value to its criticism. It has never refuted my arguments. It knows only [how] to criticise, rebuke and revile me for everything I do; and to misreport, misrepresent and pervert everything I say. Nothing that I do pleases the Congress Press. This animosity of the Congress Press towards me can to my mind, not unfairly, be explained as a reflex of the hatred of the Hindus for the Untouchables. That their animosity has become personal is clear from the fact that the Congress Press feels offended for my having criticised Mr. Jinnah, who has been the butt and the target of the Congress for the last several years.

However strong and however filthy be the abuses which the Congress Press chooses to shower on me, I must do my duty. I am no worshipper of idols. I believe in breaking them. I insist that if I hate Mr. Gandhi and Mr. Jinnah—I dislike them, I do not hate them—it is because I love India more. That is the true faith of a nationalist. I have hopes that my countrymen will some day learn that the country is greater than the men, that the worship of Mr. Gandhi or Mr. Jinnah and service to India are two very different things and may even be contradictory of each other.

15th March 1943 B.R.A.
22, Prithvi Raj Road
New Delhi

Chapter - I

I will speak of Ranade only as a public figure

I must tell you that I am not very happy over this invitation. My fear is that I may not be able to do justice to the occasion. When a year ago the Centenary of Ranade's Birthday was celebrated in Bombay the Rt. Hon'ble Srinivas Shastri was chosen to speak. For very many reasons he was well qualified for performing the duty. He can claim to be a contemporary of Ranade for a part of his life. He had seen him at close range and was an eye witness of the work to which Ranade devoted his life. He had opportunity lo judge him and compare him with his co-workers. He could therefore expound his views about Ranade with a sense of confidence and. with intimacy born out of personal touch. He could cite an anecdote and illuminate the figure of Ranade before his audience.

None of these qualifications are available to me. My connection with Ranade is of the thinnest. I had not even seen him. There are only two incidents about Ranade which I can recall. First relates to his death. I was a student in the first standard in the Satara High School. On the 16th January 1901 the High School was closed and we boys had a holiday. We asked why it was closed and we were told that because Ranade was dead. I was then about 9 years old. I knew nothing about Ranade, who he was, what he had done; like other boys I was happy over the holiday and did not care to know who died.

The second incident which reminds me of Ranade is dated much later than the first. Once I was examining some bundles of old papers belonging to my father when I found in them a paper which purported to be a petition sent by the Commissioned and non-Commissioned officers of the Mahar

Community to the Government of India against the orders issued in 1892 banning the recruitment of the Mahars in the Army. On inquiry I was told that this was a copy of a petition which was drafted by Ranade to help the aggrieved Mahars to obtain redress.

Beyond these two incidents I have nothing to recall of Ranade. My knowledge about him is wholly impersonal. It is derived from what I have read about his work and what others have said about him. You must not expect me to say anything of a personal character which will either interest you or instruct you. I propose to say what I think of him as a public man in his days and his place in Indian Politics today.

Chapter - II

Great Men" play a vital role in societal growth and renewal

As you are well aware, there are friends of Ranade who do not hesitate to describe him as a Great Man and there are others who with equal insistence deny him that place. Where does the truth lie? But this question must, I think, wait upon another, namely, is history the biography of Great Men? The question is both relevant as well as important. For, if Great Men were not the makers of history, there is no reason why we should take more notice of them than we do of cinema stars. Views differ. There are those who assert that however great a man may be, he is a creature of Time—Time called him forth, Time did everything, he did nothing. Those who hold this view, in my judgement, wrongly interpret history.

There have been three different views on the causes of historical changes. We have had the Augustinian theory of history, according to which history is only an unfolding of a divine plan in which mankind is to continue through war and suffering until that divine plan is completed at the day of judgement. There is the view of Buckle, who held that history was made by Geography and Physics. Karl Marx propounded a third view. According to him history was the result of economic forces. None of these three would admit that history is the biography of Great Men. Indeed, they deny man any place in the making of history.

No one except theologians accepts the Augustinian theory of history. As to Buckle and Marx, while there is truth in what they say, their views do not represent the whole truth. They are quite wrong in holding that impersonal forces are everything and that man is no factor in the making of history. That impersonal forces are a determining factor cannot be denied. But that the effect of impersonal forces depends on man must also be admitted. Flint may not exist everywhere. But where it does exist, it needs man to strike flint against flint to make fire. Seeds may not be found everywhere. But where they do exist, it needs man to ground it to powder and make it a delectable and nutritious paste and thereby lay the foundation of agriculture. There are many areas devoid of metals. But where they do exist, it needs a man to make instruments and machines which are the basis of civilization and culture.

Take the case of social forces. Various tragic situations arise. One such situation is of the type described by Thayer in his biography of Theodore Roosevelt when he says:

"There comes a time in every sect, party or institution when it stops growing, its arteries harden, its young men see no visions, its old men dream no dreams; it lives on the past and desperately tries to perpetuate the past. In politics when this process of petrifaction is reached we call it Bourbonism and the sure sign of the Bourbon is that, being unconscious that he is the victim of sclerosis, he sees no reason for seeking a cure. Unable to adjust himself to changed and new conditions he falls back into the past as an old man drops into his worn-out arm-chair."

The other kind of situation is not one of decay but of destruction. The possibilities of it are always present whenever there is a crisis. The old ways, old habits and old thoughts fail to lift society and lead it on. Unless new ones are found there is no possibility of survival. No society has a smooth sailing. There are periods of decay and possibilities of destruction through which every society has to pass. Some survive, some are destroyed, and some undergo stagnation and decay. Why does this happen? What is the reason that some survive? Carlyle has furnished an answer. He puts in his characteristic way:

"No time need have gone to ruin, could it have found a great enough, a man wise and good enough; Wisdom to discern truly what the Time wanted, valour to lead it on to the right road thither, these are the salvation of any Time."

This seems to me to be quite a conclusive answer to those who deny man any place in the making of history. The crisis can be met by the discovery of a new way. Where there is no new way found, society goes under. Time may suggest possible new ways. But to step on the right one is not the work of Time. It is the work of man. Man therefore is a factor in the making of history and that environmental forces whether impersonal or social if they are the first are not the last things.

Chapter - III

A Great Man must be a scourge and scavenger of society

Who can be called a Great Man? If asked of military heroes such as Alexander, Attila, Caesar and Tamerlane, the question is not difficult to answer. The military men make epochs and effect vast transitions. They appal and dazzle their contemporaries by their resounding victories. They become great without waiting to be called great. As the lion is among the deer, so they are among men. But it is equally true that their permanent effect on the history of mankind is very small. Their conquests shrink, and even so great a General as Napoleon after all his conquests left France smaller than he found it. When viewed from a distance they are seen to be only periodical, if necessary, incidents in the world's movement, leaving no permanent mark on the character of the society in which they live The details of their career and their moral may be interesting, but they do not affect Society and form no leaven to transform or temper the whole.

The answer becomes difficult when the question is asked about a person who is not a military general. For, it then becomes a question of tests, and different people have different tests.

Carlyle the apostle of Hero Worship had a test of his own. He laid it down in the following terms.

"But of Great Man especially, of him I will venture to assert that it is incredible he should have been other than true. It seems to me the primary foundation of him, this. . . No man adequate to do anything, but is first of all in right earnest about it; what I call a sincere man. I should say sincerity, a deep, great genuine sincerity, is the first characteristic of all men in any way heroic."

Carlyle was of course particular in defining his test of sincerity in precise terms, and in doing so he warned his readers by defining what his idea of sincerity was.

"Not the sincerity that calls itself sincere: ah no," he said, "that is a very poor matter indeed;— a shallow, braggart, conscious sincerity; oftenest self-conceit mainly. The Great Man's sincerity is of the kind he cannot speak of, is not conscious of: nay, I suppose, he is conscious rather of *insincerity*; for what man can walk accurately by the law of truth for one day? No, the Great Man. does not boast himself sincere, far from that; perhaps does not ask himself if he is so: I would say rather, his sincerity does not depend on himself; he cannot help being sincere!"

Lord Rosebery proposed another test when dealing with Napoleon— who was as great an Administrator as a General. In answering the question, Was Napoleon great? Rosebery used the following language:

"If by 'great' be intended the combination of moral qualities with those of intellect, great he certainty was not. But that he was great in the sense of being extraordinary and supreme we can have no doubt. If greatness stands for natural power, for predominance, for something human beyond humanity, then Napoleon was assuredly great. Besides that indefinable spark which we call genius, he represents a combination of intellect and energy which has never perhaps been equalled, never, certainly, surpassed."

There is a third test, suggested by the philosophers or, to be more accurate, by those who believe in divine guidance of human affairs. They have a different conception of what is a Great Man. To summarise the summary of their view, as given by Rosebery, a great man is launched into the world, as a great natural or supernatural force, as a scourge and a scavenger born to cleanse society and lead it on to the right path, who is engaged in a vast operation, partly positive, mainly negative, but all relating to social regeneration.

Which of these is the true test? In my judgement all arc partial and none is complete. Sincerity must be the test of a Great Man. Clemenceau once said that most statesmen are rogues. Statesmen are not necessarily Great Men, and obviously these on whose experience he founded his opinion must have been those wanting in sincerity/ Nonetheless no one can accept that sincerity is the primary or the sole test. For sincerity is not enough. A Great Man must have sincerity. For it is the sum of all moral qualities without which no man can be called great. But there must be something more than mere sincerity in a man to make him Great. A man may be sincere and yet he may be a fool, and a fool is the very antithesis of a Great Man.

A man is Great because he finds a way to save Society in its hours of crisis. But what can help him to find the way? He can do so only with the help of intellect. Intellect is the light. Nothing else can be of any avail. It is quite obvious that without the combination of sincerity and intellect no man can be great. Is this enough to constitute a Great Man? At this stage we must, I think, make a distinction between an eminent individual and a Great Man. For I am certain that a Great Man is something very different from an eminent individual. Sincerity and intellect: are enough to mark out an individual as being eminent as compared to his fellows. But they are not enough to raise him to the dignity of a Great Man.

A Great Man must have something more than what a merely eminent individual has. What must be that thing? Here comes the importance of the philosopher's definition of a Great Man. A Great Man must be motivated by the dynamics of a. social purpose and must act as the scourge and the scavenger of society. These are the elements which distinguish an eminent individual from a Great Man, and constitute his title deeds to respect and reverence.

Chapter - IV

Ranade was a devoted and courageous Social Reformer

Was Ranade a great man? He was of course great in his person. Vast in physique —he could have been called "Your Immense" as the Irish servant who could not pronounce Your Eminence used respectfully to call Cardinal Wiseman —his master. He was a man of sanguine temperament, of genial disposition and versatile in his capacity. He had sincerity which is the sum of all moral qualities and his sincerity was of the sort which was prescribed by Carlyle. It was not a conscious "braggart sincerity." It was the natural sincerity a constitutional trait and not an assumed air. He was not only big in his physique and in his sincerity, he was also big in intellect. Nobody can question that Ranade had intellect of a high calibre. He was not merely a lawyer and a judge of the High Court, he was a first class economist, a first class historian, a first class educationist, and a first class Divine. He was not a politician. Perhaps it is good that he was not. For if he had been, he might not have been a Great Man. As Abraham Lincoln said, politicians "are a set of men who have interests aside from the interests of the people and who, to say the most of them are taken as a mass, at least one long step removed from honest men."

Ranade, though not a politician, was a profound student of politics. Indeed it would be difficult to find in the history of India any man who could come up to Ranade in the width of his learning, the breadth of his wisdom and the length of his vision. There was no subject which he did not touch and in which he did not acquire profundity. His reading was on the scale of the colossal and every inch he was a scholar. He was great not merely by the standard of his Time, but he was great— measured by any standard. As I have said no claim for being a Great Man can rest on the foundation of sincerity and intellect either singly or in combination. Ranade could not be called great if he had these two qualities and no more.

His title to being a Great Man must rest upon the social purposes he served and on the way he served them. On that there can be no doubt. Ranade is known more as a social reformer than as a historian, economist or educationist. His whole life is nothing but a relentless campaign for social reform. It is on his role as a social reformer that this title to being a Great Man rests. Ranade had both the vision and the courage which the reformer needs, and in the circumstances in which he was born his vision was no small[er] a virtue than his courage. That he developed a vision of the Prophet—I am using the word in the Jewish sense—cannot but be regarded as a matter of surprise if the time in which he was born is taken into account. Ranade was born in 1842 some 24 years after the battle of Kirkee which brought the Maratha Empire to an end. The downfall of the Maratha Empire evoked different feelings among different people. There were men like Natu who served as accessories before the fact. There were some who played the part of accessories after the fact, inasmuch as they were happy that the cursed rule of the Brahmin Peshwa was brought to an end. But there can be no doubt that a large majority of the people of Maharashtra were stunned by the event.

When the whole of India was enveloped by the advancing foreign horde and its people being subjugated piece by piece, here in this little corner of Maharashtra lived a sturdy race who knew what liberty was, who had fought for it inch by inch and established it over miles and miles. By the British conquest they had lost what was to them a most precious possession. One can quite imagine how the best intellect of Maharashtra had its mind utterly confounded and its horizon fully and completely darkened. What could be the natural reaction to so great a catastrophe? Can it be other than resignation, defeatism and surrender to the inevitable? How did Ranade react? Very differently. He held out the hope that the fallen shall rise. Indeed he developed a new faith on which this hope was found[ed]. Let me quote his own words. He said:—

"I profess implicit faith in two articles of my creed. This country of ours is the true land of promise. This race of ours is the chosen race."

He did not rest quiet by merely enunciating this new Mosaic Gospel of hope and confidence. He applied his mind to the question of the realization of this hope. The first requisite was of course a dispassionate analysis of the causes of this downfall. Ranade realized that the downfall was due to certain weaknesses in the Hindu social system and unless these weaknesses were removed the hope could not be realized. The new gospel was therefore followed by a call to duty. That duty was no other than the duty to reform Hindu society.

Social reform became therefore the one dominant purpose of his life. He developed a passion for social reform and there was nothing he did not do to promote it. His methods included meetings, missions, lectures, sermons, articles, interviews, letters—all carried on with an unrelenting zeal. He established many societies. He founded many journals. But he was not content with this. He wanted something more permanent, something more systematic for promoting the cause of social reform. So he founded the Social Conference, an All-India Organization which ran as an adjunct to the Indian National Congress. Year after year the Conference met to discuss the social ills and to find the ways of remedying them, and year after year Ranade attended its annual sessions as though it was a pilgrimage and fostered the cause of social reform.

In fostering the cause of social reform Ranade showed great courage. Many people of this generation will perhaps laugh at such a claim. Courting prison has become an act of martyrdom in India. It is regarded both as a patriotic act and also as an act of courage. Most people who would otherwise be beneath notice and in whose case it could rightly be said that they were scoundrels who had taken to politics as their last refuge, have by going to prison become martyrs and have acquired a name and fame which, to say the least, is quite astounding. There would be some substance in this view, if prison life involved the rigours to which men like Tilak and those of his generation had been subjected. Prison life today has lost all its terrors. It has become a mere matter of detention. Political prisoners are no longer treated as criminals. They are placed in a separate class. There are no hardships to suffer, there is no reputation to lose and there is no privation to undergo. It calls for no courage.

But even when prison life had, as in the time of Mr. Tilak, its rigours the political prisoners could make no claim to greater courage than a Social Reformer. Most people do not realize that society can practise tyranny and oppression against an individual in a far greater degree than a Government can. The means and scope that are open to society for oppression are more extensive than those that are open to Government, also they are far more effective. What punishment in the penal code is comparable in its magnitude and its severity to excommunication? Who has greater courage—the Social

Reformer who challenges society and invites upon himself excommunication or the political prisoner who challenges Government and incurs sentence of a few months or a few years imprisonment? There is also another difference which is often lost sight of in estimating the courage shown by the social reformer and the political patriot. When the Social Reformer challenges Society there is nobody to hail him a martyr. There is nobody even to befriend him. He is loathed and shunned. But when the political patriot challenges Government he has whole society to support him. He is praised, admired and elevated as the saviour. Who shows more courage—the Social Reformer who fights alone, or the Political Patriot who fights under the cover of [a] vast mass of supporters? It would be idle to deny that Ranade showed courage in taking up the cause of Social Reform. Indeed he showed a high degree of courage. For let it be rememberedthat he lived in times when Social and Religious customs, however gross and unmoral, were regarded as sacrosanct, and when any doubt questioning their divine and moral basis was regarded not merely as heterodoxy, but as intolerable blasphemy and sacrilege.

Chapter - V

Ranade knew that reform of the Caste System was an urgent need

His path as a Reformer was not smooth. It was blocked from many sides. The sentiments of the people whom he wanted to reform were deeply rooted in the ancient past. They held the belief that their ancestors were the wisest and the noblest of men, and the social system which they had devised was of the most ideal character. What appeared to Ranade to be the shames and wrongs of the Hindu Society were to them the most sacred injunctions of their religion. This was the attitude of the common man. The intelligentsia. was divided into two schools—a school which was orthodox in its belief but unpolitical in its outlook, and a school which was modem in its beliefs but primarily political in its aims and objects. The former was led by Mr. Chiplunkar and the latter by Mr. Tilak. Both combined against Ranade and created as many difficulties for him as they could. They not only did the greatest harm to the cause of social reform, but as experience shows they have done the greatest harm to the cause of political reform in India.

The unpolitical or the orthodox school believed in the Hegelian view—it is a puzzle to me—namely to realize the ideal and idealize the real. In this it. was egregiously wrong. The Hindu Religious and Social system is such that you cannot go forward to give its ideal form a reality because the ideal is bad; nor can you attempt to elevate the real to the status of the ideal because the real. i.e., the existing state of affairs, is worse than worse could be. This is no exaggeration. Take the Hindu Religious System or take the Hindu Social System, and examine it from the point of social utility and social justice. It is said that religion is good when it is fresh from the mint. But Hindu religion has been a bad coin to start with. The Hindu ideal of society as prescribed by Hindu religion has acted as a most demoralizing and degrading influence on Hindu Society. It is Nietzschean in its form and essence.

Long before Nietzsche was born, Manu had proclaimed the gospel which Nietzsche sought to preach. It is a religion which is not intended to establish liberty, equality and fraternity. It is a gospel which proclaims the worship of the superman—the Brahamin—by the rest of the Hindu Society. It propounds that the superman and his class alone are born to live and to rule. Others are born to serve them, and to nothing more. They have no life of their own to live, and no right to develop their own personality. This has been the gospel of the Hindu Religion. Hindu philosophy, whether it is Vedanta, Sankhya, Nyaya, [or] Vaishashika, has moved in its own circle without in any way affecting the Hindu religion It has never had the courage to challenge this gospel. That Hindu philosophy that everything is Brahma remained only a matter of intellect. It never became a social philosophy. The Hindu philosophers had. both their philosophy and their Manu held apart in two hands, the right not knowing what the left had. The Hindu is never troubled by their inconsistency.

As to their social system, can things be worst[=worse]? The Caste System is in itself a degenerate form of the Chaturvarna which is the ideal of the Hindu. How can anybody who is not a congenital idiot accept Chaturvarna as the ideal form of society? Individually and socially it is a folly and a crime. One class and one class alone to be entitled to education and learning! One class and one class alone to be entitled to Arms! One class and one class alone to trade! One class and one class alone to serve! For the individual the consequences are obvious. Where can you find a learned man who has no means of livelihood who will not degrade his education? Where can you find a soldier with no education and culture who will use his arms to conserve and not to destroy? Where can you find a merchant with nothing but the acquisitive instinct to follow who will not descend to the level of the brute? Where can you find the servant who is not to acquire education, who is not to own Arms, and who is not to possess other means of livelihood, to be a man as his Maker intended him to be?

If baneful to the individual, it makes society vulnerable. It is not enough for a social structure to be good for a fair weather. It must be able to weather the storm. Can the Hindu Caste System stand the gale and the wind of an aggression? It is obvious that it cannot. Either for defence or for offence a society must be able to mobilize its forces. With functions and duties exclusively distributed and immutably assigned, what way is there for mobilization? Ninety per cent of the Hindus— Brahmins, Vaishyas and Shudras—could not bear arms under the Hindu social system. How can a country be defended if its army cannot be increased in the hour of its peril? It is not Buddha who, as is often alleged, weakened Hindu Society by his gospel of non-violence. It is the Brahminic theory of Chaturvarna that ha.s been responsible not only for the defeat, but for the decay, of Hindu Society.

Some of you will take offence at what I have said about the demoralizing effect of the Hindu socio-religious ideal on Hindu Society. But what is the truth? Can the charge be denied? Is there any society in the world which has unapproachable,, unshadowables, and unseeables? is there any society which has got a population of Criminal Tribes? Is there a society in which there exist today primitive people, who live in jungles, who do not know even to clothe themselves? How many do they count in numbers? Is it a matter of hundreds, is it a matter of thousands? I wish they numbered a paltry few. The tragedy is that they have to be counted in millions, millions of Untouchables, millions of Criminal Tribes, millions of Primitive Tribes!! One wonders whether the Hindu civilization is civilization, or infamy.

This is about the ideal. Turn now to the state of things as it existed when Ranade came on the scene. It is impossible to realize now the state of degradation they had reached when the British came on the scene, and with which the reformers like Ranade were faced. Let me begin with the condition of the intellectual class. The rearing and guiding of a civilization must depend upon its intellectual class—upon the lead given by the Brahmins. Under the old Hindu Law the Brahmin enjoyed the benefit of the clergy and could not be hanged even if he was guilty of murder, and the East India Company allowed him the privilege till 1817. That is no doubt because he was the salt of the Earth. Was there any salt left in him? His profession had lost all its nobility. He had become a pest.

The Brahmin systematically preyed on society and profiteered in religion. The *Purana*s and *Shastra*s which lie manufactured in tons are a treasure trove of sharp practices which the Brahmins employed to befool, beguile and swindle the common mass of poor, illiterate, and superstitious Hindus. It is impossible in this address to give references to them. I can only refer to the coercive measures which the Brahmins had sanctified as proper to be employed against the Hindus, to the encashment of their rights and privileges. Let those who want to know read the preamble to Regulation XXI of 1795. According to it, whenever a Brahmin wanted to get anything which could not be willingly got from his victim, he resorted to various coercive practices—lacerating his own body with knives and razors, or threatening to swallows some poison, were the usual tricks he practised to carry out his selfish purposes. There were other ways employed by the Brahmin to coerce the Hindus, which were as extraordinary as they were shameless. A common practice was the erection in front of the house of his victim of the *koorh*—a circular enclosure in which a pile of wood was placed; within the enclosure an old woman was placed, ready to be burnt in the *koorh* if his object was not granted. The second device of such a kind was the placing of his women and children in the sight of his victim and threaten[ing] to behead them. The third was the*dhurna*—starving on the doorstep of the victim.

This is nothing. Brahmins had started making claims for a right to deflower the women of non-Brahmins. The practice prevailed in the family of the Zamorin of Calicut, and among the Vallabhachari sect of Vaishnavas. What depths of degradation the Brahmins had fallen to! If, as the Bible says, the salt has lost its flavour, wherewith shall it be salted? No wonder the Hindu Society had its moral bonds loosened to a dangerous point. The East India Company had in 1819 to pass a Regulation (VII of 1819) to put a stop to this moral degeneracy. The preamble to the Regulation says that women were employed wholesale to entice and take away the wives or female children for purposes of prostitution, and it was common practice among husbands and fathers to desert their families and children. Public conscience there was none, and in the absence of conscience it was futile to expect moral indignation against the social wrongs. Indeed the Brahmins were engaged in defending every wrong for the simple reason that they lived on them. They defended Untouchability which condemned millions to the lot of the helot. They defended caste, they defended female child marriage and they defended enforced widowhood—the two great props of the Caste system. They defended the burning of widows, and they defended the social system of graded inequality with its rule of hypergamy which led the Rajputs to kill in their thousands the daughters that were born to them. What shames! What wrongs! Can such a Society show its face before civilized nations? Can such a society hope to survive? Such were the questions which Ranade asked. He concluded that on only one condition it could be saved—namely, rigorous social reform.

Chapter - VI

The "Politicals" thought that social reform was secondary

His greatest opponents however came from the political school of the intelligentsia. These politicals developed a new thesis. According to that thesis political reform was to have precedence over social reform. The thesis was argued from platform to platform and was defended by eminent people like Mr. Justice Telang, a Judge of the Bombay High Court, with the consummate skill of an acute lawyer. The thesis caught the imagination of the people. If there was one single cause to which the blocking of the Social Reform movement could be attributed, it was this cry of political reform. The thesis is unsupportable, and I have no doubt that the opponents of Ranade were wrong and, in pursuing it, did not serve the best interests of the country. The grounds on which Mr. Justice Telang defended the Politicians' thesis were of course logical. But he totally forgot that logic is not reason, and analogy is not argument. Neither did he have a correct understanding of the inter-relation between the "social" and the "political" which Ranade had.

Let us examine the reasons for the thesis. Those that were advanced were not very impressive. But I am prepared to meet the most impressive arguments that could be advanced. Even then the thesis will not stand. The following strike me as being the most impressive. In the first place, it could be said that we want political power first because we want to protect the rights of the people. This answer proceeds from a very frugal theory of Government as was propounded by the American statesman Jefferson, according to whom politics was only an affair of policing by the State so that that the rights of people were maintained without disturbance. Assume that the theory is a sound one. The question is, what is there for the State to police if there are no rights? Rights must exist before policing becomes a serious matter of substance. The thesis that political reform should precede social reform becomes on the face of it an absurd proposition, unless the idea is that the Government is to protect those who have vested rights and to penalize those who have none.

The second ground that could be urged in support of the thesis is that they wanted political power because they wanted to confer on each individual certain fundamental rights by law, and that such conferring of the political rights could not lake place unless there was political power first obtained. This of course sounds very plausible. But is there any substance in it? The idea of fundamental rights has become a familiar one since their enactment in the American Constitution and in the Constitution framed by Revolutionary France. The idea of making a gift of fundamental rights to every individual is no doubt very laudable. The question is how to make them effective. The prevalent. view is that once rights are enacted in a law, then they are safeguarded. This again is an unwarranted assumption.

As experience proves, rights are protected not by law but by the social and moral conscience of society. If [the] social conscience is such that it is prepared to recognize the rights which law chooses to enact, rights will be safe and secure. But if the fundamental rights are opposed by the community, no Law, no Parliament, no judiciary can guarantee them in the real sense of the word. What is the use of the fundamental rights to the Negroes in America., to the Jews in Germany, and to the Untouchables in India? As Burke said, there is no method found for punishing the multitude. Law can punish a single solitary recalcitrant criminal. It can never operate against a whole body of people who are determined to defy it. Social conscience—to use the language of Coleridge—that calm incorruptible legislator of the soul without whom all other powers would "meet in mere oppugnancy—is the only safeguard of all rights fundamental or non-fundamental."

The third argument of the Politicals could be based on the right to self-government. That self-government is better than good government is a well-known cry. One cannot give it more value than one can give to a slogan, and all would like to be assured that self-government would also be a good government. There is no doubt that the Politicals wanted good government, and their aim was to establish a democratic form of government. But they never stopped to consider whether a democratic form of government was possible. Their contention was founded on a series of fallacies. A Democratic form of government presupposes a Democratic form of society. The formal framework of Democracy is of no value, and would indeed be a misfit if there was no social democracy. The politicals never realized that democracy was not a form of government. It was essentially a form of Society.

It may not be necessary for a Democratic society to be marked by unity, by community of purpose, by loyalty to public ends, and by mutuality of sympathy. But it does unmistakably involve two things. The first is an attitude of mind, an attitude of respect and equality towards their fellows. The second is a social organization free from rigid social barriers. Democracy is incompatible and inconsistent with isolation and exclusiveness, resulting in the distinction between the privileged and the unprivileged. Unfortunately, the opponents of Ranade were never able to realize the truth of this fact.

Chapter - VII

Ranade was right to make social reform an urgent priority

One may judge it by any test, and it will be found that the stand that Ranade took in this controversy, and his plan of work, were correct and fundamental to—if they were not the pre-requisites of—political reform. Ranade argued that there were no rights in the Hindu Society which the moral sense of man could recognize. There were privileges and disabilities, privileges for a few and disabilities for a vast majority. Ranade struggled to create rights. Ranade wanted to vitalize the conscience of the Hindu Society, which had become moribund as well morbid. Ranade aimed to create a real social democracy, without which there could be no sure and stable politics. The conflict was between two opposing points of view, and it centred round the question which is more important for the survival of a nation, political freedom or strong moral fibre. Ranade took the view that moral stamina was more important than political freedom. This was also the view of Lecky, the great historian who after a careful and comparative study of history came to the conclusion that.

"The foundation of a Nation's strength and prosperity is laid in pure domestic life, in commercial integrity, in a high standard of moral worth, and of public spirit, in a simple habits, in courage, uprightness, and a certain soundness and moderation of judgement which springs quite as much from character as from intellect. If you would form a wise judgement of the future of a nation, observe carefully whether these qualities are increasing or decaying. Observe carefully what qualities count for most in public life. Is character becoming of greater or less importance? Are the men who obtain the highest posts in the nation men of whom, in private life, irrespective of party competent judges speak with genuine respect? Are they of sincere convictions, consistent lives and indisputable integrity? It is by observing this current that you can best cast the horoscope of a nation."

Ranade was not only wise, but he was also logical. He told [=warned] his opponents against playing the part of Political Radicals and Social Tories. In clear and unmistakable terms he warned them saying.

"You canned be liberal by halves. You cannot be liberal in politics and conservative in religion. The heart and the head must go together. You cannot cultivate your intellect, enrich your mind, enlarge the sphere of your political rights and privileges, and at the same time keep your hearts closed and cramped. It is an idle dream to expect men to remain enchained and enshackled in their own superstition and social evils, while they are struggling hard to win rights and privileges from their rulers. Before long these vain dreamers will find their dreams lost."

Experience has shown that these words of Ranade have been true, even prophetic. Let those who deny this consider: Where are we today in politics, and why are we where we are? It is now 50 years since the National Congress was born. Its stewardship has passed hands, I won't say from the sane to the insane, or from realists to idealists, but from moderates to radicals. Where does the country stand today at the end of 50 years of political marching? What is the cause of this deadlock? The answer is simple. The cause of deadlock is the absence of Communal settlement. Ask why is communal settlement necessary for political settlement, and you realize the fundamental importance of the stand that Ranade took. For the answer to this question is to be found in the wrong social system, which is too undemocratic, too over-weighed in favour of the classes and against the masses, too class-conscious and too communally-minded. Political democracy would become a complete travesty if it were built upon its foundations.

That is why nobody except the high-caste Hindus will agree to make it the case of a political Democracy without serious adjustments. Well may some people argue to their satisfaction that the deadlock is the creation of the British Government. People like to entertain thoughts which soothe them and which throw responsibility on others. This is the psychology of escapism. But it cannot alter the fact that it is the defects of [the] social system which has [=have] given rise to the communal problem and which has [=have] stood in the way of India getting political power.

Ranade's aim was to cleanse the old order, if not to build a new one. He insisted on improving the moral tone of Hindu Society. If he had been heard and followed, the system would have at least lost its rigours and its rigidity. If it could not have avoided Communal settlement, it would have made it easy. For his attempts, limited as they were, would have opened the way to mutual trust. But the Politicals had developed a passion for politicalpower which had so completely blinded them that they refused to see virtue in anything else. Ranade has had his revenge. Is not the grant of political safeguard[s] a penalty for denying the necessity of social Reform?

How much did Ranade achieve in the field in which he played so dominant a part? In a certain sense the question is not very important. Achievement is never the true measure of greatness. "Alas," as Carlyle said, "we know very well that ideals can never be completely embodied in practice. Ideals must ever lie a very great way off; and we will right thankfully content ourselves with any not intolerable approximation thereto!" Let no man, as Schillar says, too querulously "measure by a scale of perfection the meagre product of reality" in this poor world of ours. We will esteem him no wise man; we will esteem him a sickly discontented foolish man. And yet Ranade's record of achievement was not altogether bare.

The problems facing the then Social Reformers contained in the statement on Social Reform prepared by Rai Bahadur P. Anandcharly were five: (1) Early marriage; (2) Remarriages of widows; (3) Liberty for our countrymen to travel—or sojourn in foreign lands; (4) Women's rights of property; and (5) Education of women. Of this programme he achieved a great part. If he did not achieve all, there were the odds against him, which should never be forgotten. A clever, [a] determined, and an insincere intelligentsia came forward to defend orthodoxy and give battle to Ranade. The scenes were exciting, as exciting as those of a dread grim [sic] of battle. And battle it was. One cannot recall the spirit of the time when this controversy over social reform was raging in this country. It is not possible for decency to enter into the abuses that were hurled, the calumnies that were uttered, the strategies that were employed by the orthodox section against the Social Reformers. It is impossible to read the writing of those who supported orthodoxy in their opposition to the Age of Consent Bill without realizing the depth of the degradation to which the so-called leaders of the peoples had fallen.

The Bill aimed to punish a husband who would have sexual intercourse with his wife if she had not attained the age of 12. Could any sane man, could any man with a sense of shame, oppose so simple a measure? But it was opposed, and Ranade had to bear the brunt of the mad orthodoxy. Assuming that Ranade's achievements were small; who could take pride or exultation in his failure to achieve more? There was no cause for exultation. The decline of Social Reform was quite natural. The odium of Social Reform was too great. The appeal of political power too alluring. The result was that social reform found fewer and fewer adherents. In course of time the platform of the Social Reform Conference was deserted, and men flocked to the Indian National Congress. The politicians triumphed over the Social Reformers. I am sure that nobody will now allow that their triumph was a matter for pride. It is certainly a matter of sorrow. Ranade may not have been altogether on the winning side, but he was not on the wrong side and certainly never on the side of the wrong as some of his opponents were.

Chapter - VIII

Ranade showed none of the heedless egotism of Gandhi and Jinnah

How does Ranade compare with others? Comparisons are always odious and unpleasant. At the same time it is true that there is nothing more illuminating than comparisons. Of course, in making them one must bear in mind that to be interesting and instructive, comparisons must be between those that are alike. Fortunately there is [a] field for comparison. Ranade was a Social Reformer, and as a Social Reformer he could be usefully compared with other Social Reformers. Particularly illuminating will be the comparison between Ranade and Jotiba Phule. Phule was born in 1827 and died in 1890. Ranade was born in 1842 and died in 1901. Thus Phule and Ranade were contemporaries, and both were [among the] foremost social reformers. Some may perhaps demur to [=doubt] the wisdom of comparing Ranade with other politicians. This can only be on the ground that Ranade was not a politician. To say that Ranade was not a politician is to impose a very narrow and very restricted meaning upon the term politician. A politician does not merely trade in politics, but he also represents a particular faith covering both—the method as well as the metaphysics of politics. Ranade was the founder of a school of politics which was distinctive for its method as well as for metaphysics. Used in this sense, Ranade was a politician and could be usefully compared with other politicians. Comparisons of Ranade with social reformers and with politicians cannot but be illuminating, and there is enough material for such comparisons. The question really is one of time and taste. Time will not permit any extensive comparison of Ranade being made both with social reformers as well as with politicians. I must really choose between comparing Ranade with social reformers or with politicians. This is a matter of taste.

Left to myself I would have preferred to use my available time to compare Ranade with Phule. For I regard Social Reform [as] more fundamental than political reform. Unfortunately my taste is different from the taste of the audience, and I feel that in detaining the audience I must be guided more by its likes and dislikes than my own. The ardour for social reform has cooled down. The craze for politics has held the Indian public in its grip. Politics has become an appetiser—a mastic [such that] the more one tastes it the more one craves it. The task I am undertaking is a very unpleasant one, and if I venture upon it, it is only because it is my duty to expound fully, and the desire of the public to know truly, the value of Ranade's political philosophy and his place among politicians of today.

Who are the present-day politicians with whom Ranade is to be compared? Ranade was a great politician of his day. He must therefore be compared with the greatest of today. We have on the horizon of India two Great Men, so big that they could be identified without being named—Gandhi and Jinnah. What sort of a history they will make may be a matter for posterity to tell. For us it is enough that they do indisputably make headlines for the Press. They hold leading strings. One leads the Hindus, the other leads the Muslims. They are the idols and heroes of the hour. I propose to compare them with Ranade. How do they compare with Ranade? It is necessary to make some observations upon their temperaments and methods, with which they have now familiarized us. I can give only my impressions of them, for what they are worth.

The first thing that strikes me is that it would be difficult to find two persons who would rival them for their colossal egotism, to whom personal ascendancy is everything and the cause of the country a mere counter on the table. They have made Indian politics a matter of personal feud. Consequences have no terror for them; indeed they do not occur to them until they happen. When they do happen they either forget the cause, or if they remember it, they overlook it with a complacency which saves them from any remorse. They choose to stand on a pedestal of splendid isolation. They wall themselves off from their equals. They prefer to open themselves to their inferiors. They are very unhappy at and impatient of criticism, but are very happy to be fawned upon by flunkeys. Both have developed a wonderful stagecraft, and arrange things in such a way that they are always in the limelight wherever they go.

Each of course claims to be supreme. If supremacy was their only claim, it would be a small wonder. In addition to supremacy each claims infallibility for himself. Pius IX, during whose sacred regime as Pope the issue of infallibility was raging, said— "Before I was Pope I *believed* in Papal infallibility, now I *feel* it." This is exactly the attitude of the two leaders whom Providence—may I say, in his unguarded moments—has appointed to lead us. This feeling of supremacy and infallibility is strengthened by the Press. One cannot help saying that. The language used by Gardiner to describe the Northcliffe brand of journalism, in my opinion, quite appropriately describes the present state of journalism in India.

Journalism in India was once a profession. It has now become a trade. It has no more moral function than the manufacture of soap. It does not regard itself as the responsible adviser of the Public. To give the news uncoloured by any motive, to present a certain view of public policy which it believes to be for the good of the community, to correct and chastise without fear all those, no matter how high, who have chosen a wrong or a barren path, is not regarded by journalism in India its first or foremost duty. To accept a hero and worship him has become its principal duty. Under it, news gives place to sensation, reasoned opinion to unreasoning passion, appeal to the minds of responsible people to appeal to the emotions of the irresponsible. Lord Salisbury spoke of the Northcliffe journalism as written by office-boys for office-boys. Indian journalism is all that plus something more. It is written by drum-boys to glorify their heroes. Never has the interest of country been sacrificed so senselessly for the propagation of hero-worship. Never has hero-worship become so blind as we see it in India today. There are, I am glad to say, honourable exceptions. But they are too few, and their voice is never heard.

Entrenched behind the plaudits of the Press, the spirit of domination exhibited by these two Great Men has transgressed all limits. By their domination they have demoralised their followers and demoralized politics. By their domination they have made half their followers fools and the other half hypocrites. In establishing their supremacy they have taken the aid of "big business" and money magnates. For the first time in our country, money is taking the field as an organised power.

The questions which President Roosevelt propounded for [the] American Public to consider will arise here, if they have not already arisen: Who shall rule—wealth, or man? Which shall lead, money or intellect? Who shall fill public stations, educated and patriotic free men, or the feudal serfs of corporate Capital? For the present, Indian politics, at any rate the Hindu part of it, instead of being spiritualised has become grossly commercialised, so much so that it has become a byword for corruption. Many men of culture are refusing to concern themselves in this cesspool.

Politics has become a kind of sewage system, intolerably unsavoury and unsanitary. To become a politician is like going to work in the drain.

Politics in the hands of these two Great Men have become a competition in extravaganza. If Mr. Gandhi is known as Mahatma, Mr. Jinnah must be known as Qaid-i-Azim. If Gandhi has the Congress, Mr. Jinnah must have the Muslim League. If the Congress has a Working Committee and the All-India Congress Committee, the Muslim League must have its Working Committee and its Council. The session of the Congress must be followed by a session of the League. If the Congress issues a statement, the League must also follow suit. If the Congress passes a Resolution of 17,000 words, the Muslim League's Resolution must exceed it by at least a thousand words. If the Congress President has a Press Conference, the Muslim League President must have his. If the Congress must address an: appeal to the United Nations, the Muslim League must not allow itself to be outbidden.

When is all this to end? When is there to be a settlement? There are no near prospects. They will not meet, except on preposterous conditions. Jinnah insists that Gandhi should admit that he is a Hindu. Gandhi insists that Jinnah should admit that he is one of the leaders of the Muslims. Never has there been such a deplorable state of bankruptcy of statesmanship as one sees in these two leaders of India. They are making long and interminable speeches, like lawyers whose trade it is to contest everything, concede nothing, and talk by the hour. Suggest anything by way of solution for the deadlock to either of them, and it is met by an everlasting "Nay." Neither will consider a solution of the problems which is not eternal. Between them Indian politics has become "frozen," to use a well-known Banking phrase, and no political action is possible.

How does Ranade strike [us], as compared to these two? I have no personal impression to give. But reading what others have said, I think I can say what he must have been like. He had not a tinge of egotism in him. His intellectual attainments could have justified any amount of pride, nay even insolence. But he was the most modest of men. Serious youths were captivated by his learning and geniality. Many, feeling completely under his sway, responded to his ennobling influence, and moulded their whole lives with the passionate reverence for their adored master. He refused to be satisfied with the praises of fools, and was never afraid of moving in the company of equals and of the give and take it involves. He never claimed to be a mystic relying on the inner voice. He was a rationalist, prepared to have his views tested in the light of reason and experience. His greatness was natural. He needed no aid of the stage, nor the technique of an assumed eccentricity, nor the means of a subsidized press. As I said, Ranade was principally a Social Reformer. He was not a politician in the sense of one who trades in politics. But he has played an important part in the political advancement of India. To some of the politicians he acted as the teacher who secured such signal successes, and who dazzled their critics by their brilliance. To some he acted as the guide, but to all he acted as the philosopher.

What was the political philosophy of Ranade? It may be summed up in three propositions :

(1) We must not set up as our ideal something which is purely imaginary. An ideal must be such that it must carry the assurance that it is a practicable one.

(2) In politics, sentiment and temperament of the people are more important than intellect and theory. This is particularly so in the matter of framing a Constitution. A Constitution is as much a matter of taste as clothes are. Both must fit, both must please.

(3) In political negotiations, the rule must be what is possible. That does not mean that we should be content with what is offered. No. It means that you must not refuse what is offered when you know that your sanctions are inadequate to compel your opponent to concede more.

These are the three main doctrines of Ranade's political philosophy. It would be quite easy to illustrate them by appropriate quotations from his writings and his speeches. There is no time for that, nor is there any necessity, for they must be clear to every student of Ranade's speeches and writings. Who could quarrel with Ranade on these three propositions, and if there be one, on which? On the first only a visionary will quarrel. We need not take any notice of him. The second proposition is so evident that we could only ignore it at our peril. The third proposition is something on which a difference of opinion is possible. Indeed it is this which divided the Liberals from the Congressmen. I am not a liberal, but I am sure the view Ranade held was the right one. There can be no compromise on principle, and there should not be. But once the principle is agreed upon, there can be no objection to realize it by instalments. Graduation in politics is inevitable, and when the principle is accepted it is not harmful and indeed it may in certain circumstances be quite advantageous.

On this third proposition there was really no difference between him and Tilak, except this: Tilak would have the possible maximised by the application of sanctions; Ranade would look askance at sanctions. This is all. On the rest they were agreed. The absence of sanctions in Ranade's political philosophy need not detract much from its worth. We all know what sanctions are available to us. We have tried all, old as well as new, with what effect I need not stop to describe.

Chapter - IX

Ranade's moderate, thoughtful views were politically sound

In celebrating the birthday of Ranade we must not overlook what the critics and opponents are likely to say. The critics will ask what is the point in celebrating the birthday of Ranade. That the days of hero-worship are gone long past, will be the line of their argument. The opponents will say if I condemn idolatry when it pertains to Mr. Gandhi and to Mr. Jinnah, how do I join in idolizing Mr. Ranade? These are very pertinent questions. True hero-worship is dying. Of that there is no doubt. It was dying even in the days of Carlyle who indignantly complained against his age, saying.

"This is an age that as it were denies the existence of Great Men: denies the inevitableness of great men."

"Show our critics a great man," he said, and "They begin to what they ca ll 'account for him'; not to worship him but take the dimensions of him."

But hero-worship is certainly not dead in India. India is still par excellence the land of idolatry. There is idolatry in religion, there is idolatry in politics. Heroes and hero-worship is a hard, if unfortunate, fact in India's political life. I agree that hero-worship is demoralizing for the devotee and dangerous to the country. I welcome the criticism, in so far as it conveys a caution that you must know that your man is really great before you start worshipping him. This unfortunately is not an easy task. For in these days, with the Press in hand, it is easy to manufacture Great Men. Carlyle used a happy phrase when he described the great men of history as so many Bank Notes. Like Bank Notes they represent gold. What we have to see [=verify] is that they are not forged notes. I admit that we ought to be more cautious in our worship of great men. For in this country we have perhaps arrived at such a stage when alongside the notice boards saying "beware of pickp - ockets" we need to have notice boards saying "beware of Great Men." Even Carlyle, who defended the worship of Great Men, warned his readers how.

"Multitudes of Men have figured in history as Great Men who were false and selfish." He regretted deeply that "The World's wages (of homage) are pocketed (by these so-called Great Men), the World's work is not done. Heroes have gone out; quacks have come in."

Ranade never received the honours of apotheosis as these great men of India today are destined to receive. How could he? He did not come with a message hot from Senai. He performed no miracles and promised no speedy deliverance and splendour. He was not a genius and he had no superhuman qualities. But there are compensations. If Ranade did not show splendour and dominance, he brought us no catastrophe. If he had no superhuman qualities to use in the service of India, India was saved from ruin by its [=their] abuse. If he was not a genius, he did not display that perverse super-subtlety of intellect, and a temper of mind which is fundamentally dishonest and which has sown the seeds of distrust and which has made settlement so difficult of achievement.

There is nothing exuberant and extravagant in Ranade. He refused to reap cheap notoriety by playing the part of an extremist. He refused to mislead people by playing upon and exploiting the patriotic sentiments of the people. He refused to be a party to methods which are crude, which have volume but no effect, and which are neither fool-proof nor knave-proof, and which break the back even of the most earnest and sincere servants of the country and disable them from further effort. In short, Ranade was like the wise Captain who knows that his duty is not to play with his ship clever and masterful tricks, just for effect and show in the midst of the ocean, but to take it safely to its appointed port. In short, Ranade was not a forged bank note and in worshipping him we have no feeling of kneeling before anything that is false.

In the second place ,this celebration of Ranade's birthday is not all an act of hero-worship. Hero-worship in the sense of expressing our unbounded admiration is one thing. To obey the hero is a totally different kind of hero-worship. There is nothing wrong in the former, while the latter is no doubt a most pernicious thing. The former is only man's respect for everything which is noble and of which the great man is only an embodiment. The latter is the villain's [=peasant's] fealty to his lord. The former is consistent with respect, but the latter is a sign of debasement. The former does not take away one's intelligence to think and independence to act. The latter makes one a perfect fool. The former involves no disaster to the State. The latter is the source of positive danger to it. In short, in celebrating Ranade's birthday we are not worshipping a boss who is elected by no one, accountable to no one, and removable by no one, but paying our tribute of admiration to a leader who led and did not drive people, who sought to give effect to their deliberate judgement and did not try to impose his own will upon them by trickery or by violence.

In the third place, it is not for hero-worship for which this gathering has assembled. This is an occasion to remind ourselves of the political philosophy of Ranade. To my mind it has become necessary to remind ourselves of it from time to time. For his is a philosophy which is safe and sound, sure if slow. Even if it does not glitter, it is none the less gold. Do any have doubt? If they have, let them ponder over the following utterances of Bismark, Balfour, and Morley. Bismark the great German Statesman said.

"Politics is the game of the possible." Balfour in his Introduction to Walter Bagehot's well-known book on the English Constitution says.

"If we would find the true basis of the long drawn process which has gradually converted medieval monarchy into a modern democracy, the process by which so much has been changed and so little destroyed, we must study temperament and character rather than intellect and theory. This is a truth which those who recommend the wholesale adoption of British Institutions in strange lands might remember with advantage. Such an experiment can hardly be without its dangers. Constitutions are easily copied; temperaments are not; and if it should happen that the borrowed constitution and the native temperament fail to correspond, the misfit may have serious results. It matters little what other gifts a people may possess if they are wanting in these which, from this point of view, are of most importance. If, for example, they have no capacity for grading their loyalties as well as for being moved by them; if they have no natural inclination to liberty and no natural respect for law; if they lack good humour and tolerate foul play; if they know not how to compromise or when; if they have not that distrust of extreme conclusions which is sometimes misdescribed as want of logic; if corruption does not repel them; and if their divisions tend to be either too numerous or too profound, the successful working of British Institutions may be difficult or impossible. It may indeed be least possible where the arts of Parliamentary persuasion and the dexterities of party management are brought to their highest perfection."

Morley has observed.

"To hurry on after logical perfection is to show one's self-ignorant of the material of that social structure with which the politician has to deal. To disdain anything short of an organic change in thought or institution is infatuation. To be willing to make such changes too frequently, even when they are possible, is foolhardiness. That fatal French saying about small reforms being the worst enemies of great reforms is, in the sense in which it is commonly used, a formula of social ruin." These are the principles on which success in Politics depends. Are they different from those which Ranade enunciated? It bespeaks greatness in Ranade that he should have propounded them years before Bismark, Balfour and Morley.

The generation which Ranade served was wise in taking him as its political guide, friend and philosopher. His greatness lies in the fact that he can be a guide, friend and philosopher to this present, nay even to future generations.

There is one charge against Ranade which is frequently made and which I think must be met. It is said of Ranade that he believed that the conquest of India by the British was Providential, that it was in the best interest of India, that she should remain within the British Empire, and that therein lay her final destiny. In short, Ranade is accused of being opposed to India's Independence.

The charge is founded on the following utterances of Ranade.

"It cannot be easily assumed that in God's Providence, such vast multitudes as those who inhabit India were placed centuries together under influences and restraints of alien domination, unless such influences and restraints were calculated to do lasting service in the building up of the strength and character of the people in directions in which the Indian races were most deficient. Of one thing we are certain, that after lasting over five hundred years, the Mohammedan Empire gave way, and made room for the re-establishment of the old native races in the Punjab, and throughout Central Hindusthan and Southern India, on foundations of a much more solid character than those which yielded so easily before the assaults of the early Mohammedan conquerors."

"Both Hindus and Mohammedans lack many of those virtues represented by the love of order and regulated authority. Both are wanting in the love of municipal freedom, in the exercise of virtues necessary for civic life, and in aptitudes for mechanical skill, in the love of science and research in the love and daring of adventurous discovery, the resolution to master difficulties, and in chivalrous respect for womankind. Neither the old Hindus nor the old Mohammedan civilization was in a condition to train these virtues in a way to bring up the races of India on a level with those of Western Europe, and so the work of education had to be renewed, and it has been now going on for the past century and more under the *Pax Brittanica* with results—which all of us are witnesses to in ourselves."

A mere glance at these statements is enough to show that the charge is based on a misunderstanding, if not on a misreading, of the statements. The statements are plain and simple, and they cannot even by inference be said to lead to the conclusion that Ranade was opposed to India's independence. In that sense the charge is false and without foundation.

These statements of Ranade, far from casting any reflection upon his self-respect, testify to his wisdom and to his sagacity. What did Ranade want to convey by these statements? As I understand them, I think Ranade wanted to convey two things. The first thing he wanted to convey was that the conquest of India by Britain has given India the time, the opportunity, and the necessary shelter for rebuilding, renovating, and repairing her economic and social structure, to refit herself for bearing the strain of any foreign aggression when she does become free. The second thing Ranade wanted to convey was that going out of the British Empire by India before she had satisfied and solidified herself into a single nation, unified in thought, in feeling, and charged with a sense of a common destiny, was to invite chaos and disruption in the name of independence.

How very important these truths are! People do not realize the part that shelter plays in the smooth working out of social, economic and political conflicts which are inevitable in every society which desires to advance. The late Prof. Maitland was once asked to explain why Parliamentary Institutions flourished in England but failed to take root in Europe. His answer reveals the importance of shelter. He said the difference was due to the English channel. By this answer what he meant to convey was that by reason of the English channel England was immune from foreign aggression while she was repairing her own body politic, and therefore it became safe for people to fight against their King for Liberty and also safe for the King to allow it to his people. This importance of shelter was also emphasized by Abraham Lincoln. In a speech devoted to showing why American Political Institutions were destined to remain perpetual, Lincoln said.

"All the armies of Europe, Asia and Africa combined. . . with a Bonaparte for a Commander, could not by force take a drink from Ohio, or make a track on the Blue Ridge in a trial of a thousand years."

In this Lincoln was also emphasizing the importance and the necessity for shelter for social reconstruction. India is not a sheltered country as England and America are. She lies across and on the roads, whether the roads are land routes, sea routes, or air routes. As she has no shelter, the fear is that she will be broken up if she is attacked from outside while she is engaged in refitting herself. India needs a dry dock as a shelter for the period of her refitting, and the British Empire is a dry dock for her. Who can say that Ranade was not wise in asking his countrymen to bear in mind the importance of a shelter which the British Empire can give and which India needs so much?

A servient [=subordinate] nation is always eager to cut the knot and declare its independence of the dominant nation. But it seldom stops to consider the effect of independence on itself. Such a consideration is however very important. It is not often realized that the knot which binds the servient nation to the dominant nation is more necessary to the servient nation than to the dominant nation. It depends upon the conditions inside the servient nation. The servient nation may be one whole. The servient nation may consist of parts. The parts may be such that they will never become one whole. Or the parts may be such that they are not yet one whole, but if held together longer they will become one whole. The effect which the cutting of the knot will have on the servient nation will depend upon the internal condition of the servient nation. There may be every good in cutting the knot by a servient nation which is one whole. Nothing good or nothing worse can happen—depends upon how one looks at it—by the cutting of the knot by a nation in which the parts can never become one whole. But there is positive danger in the third case. The premature cutting of the knot is sure to lead to disintegration, where integration is desirable and possible. It would be a wanton act. This is the second danger which Ranade wanted to caution his countrymen against.

Who can say that Ranade was not wise in giving this caution? Those who are inclined to question its necessity have only to look to China. It is 30 years since the Chinese Revolution took place. Have the Chinese settled down? No. People are still asking "when will the Chinese revolution stop revolving?" and those who know the conditions in China cannot do better than say "Perhaps in another hundred years." Has China found a stable Government having the allegiance of all Chinese? Far from it. Indeed if truth be told, China after the revolution has been a land of disunity and disruption, far more than she was ever before. The Revolution has produced a chaos of such magnitude that her very independence has been put in peril. Few Indians are aware of the fact that if China has not lost her independence as a result of the chaos caused by the Revolution, it is only because she had too many enemies who could not agree as to which of them should devour her. The Chinese Revolution was a great mistake. That was the opinion of Yuan Shih-k'ai who said.

"I doubt whether the people of China are at present ripe for a Republic or whether under present conditions a Republic is adapted to the Chinese people. . . The adoption of a limited monarchy would bring conditions back to the normal and would bring stability much more rapidly than that end could be attained through any experimental form of Government unsuited to the genius of the people or to the present conditions in China. . . My only reason for favouring the retention of the present Emperor is that I believe in a constitutional monarchy. If we are to have that form of Government, there is nobody else whom the people would agree upon for his place. My sole aim, in this crisis, is to save China from dissolution and the many evils that would follow."

Those who think that China should be rather a warning to Indians than an example will, far from accusing Ranade for [=of] opposing India's independence, will be happy that he had the wisdom to foresee the evils of a premature revolution, and warn his countrymen against taking a similar step.

Chapter - IX

Why then has Ranade's Liberal Party so clearly failed?

Posterity is always interested in the last words and last regrets of great men. The last words of great men are not always significant of their experience of this world or their vision of the next. For instance the last thoughts of Socrates were to call Crito and say, "We owe a cock to Aesculapius; discharge the debt, and by no means omit it." But their last regrets are always significant and worth pondering over. Take the case of Napoleon. Napoleon, before his death at St. Helena, showed evidence of being uneasy over three capital points which constituted his last regrets. They were: that he could not have died at some supreme moment of his career; that he left Egypt and gave up his Eastern ambitions; and last but by no means the least, his defeat at Waterloo.

Had Ranade any supreme regrets? One thing is certain: that Ranade, if he had any, could not have the same regrets such as those which disturbed the peace of mind of Napoleon. Ranade lived for service and not for glory. It mattered very little to him whether the moment of his death was glorious or inglorious, or whether he died as a hero, as a conqueror or a master, or whether he died as a common man sometimes does of common cold. As a matter of fact, Ranade was not troubled by any regrets. So far as [the] record goes, Ranade does not seem to be conscious of any act or event about which he had any regrets. He died a happy and a peaceful death. But it is worthwhile asking, could Ranade have any regrets if he came to life today? I am sure there is one matter over which he will feel extremely grieved— namely the present condition of the Liberal Party in India.

What is the present position of the Liberal Party in India? The Liberal Party is a casualty. Indeed this is a very mild expression. The Liberals are "the contemptibles" of Indian Politics. To use the language of Norton used in another connection, they are disowned by the people, unowned by the Government, having the virtues of neither, but possessing the vices of both. There was a time when the Liberal Party was the rival of the Congress. Today the relation of the Liberal Party to the Congress is that of a dog to his master. Occasionally the dog barks at his master, but for the most part of his life he is content to follow him. What is the Liberal Party if not the tail of the Congress? Many are asking, why do not the Liberals merge in the Congress—so useless has their existence become. How can Ranade help not [=help] regretting the collapse of the Liberal Party? How can any Indian help regretting it?

The collapse of the Liberal Party is a tragedy to the Liberals. But it is really a disaster to the country. The existence of a party is so essential to a popular Government that it is impossible to conceive the possibility of getting on without it. As an eminent American historian says.

"It is easier to imagine the demolition of any part of our constitutional organization, the submersion of a large part of what the Constitution describes, than to imagine our getting on without political combinations: they are our vital institutions."

Indeed, to attempt to govern a country by the mass of voters without the control and discipline of a Party is, to use the language of James Bryce.

"Like attempting to manage a rail-board by the votes of uninformed share holders, or to lay the course of a sailing ship by the votes of the passengers."

It is undeniable that a Party is an essential adjunct to Popular Government. But it is equally undeniable that the rule of a single party is fatal to Popular Government. In fact it is a negation of Popular Government. The case of Germany and Italy furnish the most cogent evidence on this point. Instead of taking a warning from the totalitarian States, we are taking them as models to copy. The one-party system is being hailed in this country in the name of national solidarity. Those who are doing so are failing to take note of the possibilitics of tyranny, as well as the possibilities of misdirection of public affairs, which is[=are] inherent in the one-party Government.

To have Popular Government run by a single Party is to let democracy become a mere form, for despotism to play its part from behind it. How under one-party Government the tyranny of the majority ceases to be an empty phrase and becomes a menacing fact has been our experience, in India, under the Congress Regime. Were we not told by Mr. Rajgopalachariar that the separation of the Executive and the Judiciary which was necessary under the British is no longer necessary? Does it not show the Despot's taste for blood? Despotism does not cease to be despotism because it is elective. Nor does despotism become agreeable because the Despots belong to our own kindred. To make it subject to election is no guarantee against despotism. The real guarantee against despotism is to confront it with the possibility of its dethronement, of its being laid low, of its being superseded by a rival party.

Every Government is liable to error of judgement, [a] great many liable to bad administration, and not a few to corruption, injustice, and acts of oppression and bad faith. No Government ought to be free from criticism. But who can criticize a Government? Left to individuals, it can never be done. Sir Toby has left behind advice as to how one should deal with one's enemy. He said: soon, "so soon as ever thou seest him, draw, and as thou drawest, swear horrible." But this is not possible for an individual who wants to stand up against a Government. There are various things against individuals' successfully playing that part.

There is in the first place what Bryce calls the fatalism of the multitude, that tendency to acquiesce and submit due to the sense of [the] insignificance of individual effort, the sense of helplessness arising from the belief that the affairs of men are swayed by large forces whose movements cannot be turned by individual effort. In the second place there is [the] possibility of the tyranny of the majority which often manifests [itself] in suppressing and subjecting to penalties and other social disabilities persons who do not follow the majority, of which some of us have good experience during the Congress regime. In the third place there is the fear of the C.I.D., the Gestapo, and all the other instrumentalities which are at the disposal of the Government to shadow its critics and to silence them.

The secret of freedom is courage, and courage is born in [the] combination of individuals into a party. A Party is necessary to run Government. But two Parties are necessary to keep Government from being a despotism. A democratic Government can remain democratic only if it is worked by two parties—a Party in power and a Party in opposition. As Jennings puts it.

"If there is no opposition there is no democracy. 'His Majesty's Opposition' is no idle phrase. His Majesty needs an opposition as well as a Government."

In the light of these considerations, who could deny [them and say] that the collapse of the Liberal Party in India is not a major disaster? Without the resuscitation of the Liberal Party or the formation of another Party, the fight for freedom will result in loss of freedom, for despotism is antithetical of freedom whether the despotism is native or foreign. It is a pity Indians have lost sight of this fact. But I have no doubt those who are shouting that the Congress is the only Party and that the Congress is the nation will live to rue their decision.

Why has the Liberal Party collapsed? Is there something wrong in the Philosophy of Ranade? Is there anything wrong with the men in the Liberal Party? Or is the working of the Liberal Party at fault? I for one hold that there is nothing fundamentally wrong with the philosophy of Ranade. Nor can it be said that of the two the Congress has the best cause and the Liberal Party the best men. The Liberal Party has both. To my mind what has brought about the collapse of the Liberal Party is the complete lack of organization.

It may not be without interest to expose the weaknesses in the organization of the Liberal Party.

As pointed out by Pendleton Herring in his volume on *Politics of Democracy*, the organization of a Party is spread over three concentric rings. The centre ring represents the oligarchy in control of the party organization—what is called the High Command. There are associated with it, its workers who are primarily concerned with securing their livelihood through the party organization, whether as party officials or through public office. They are called professional politicians, and constitute the party machine. Surrounding this inner group—the High Command and the machine—there is a large circle of persons bound to the Party by ties of tradition and emotional loyalty. They think of the principles professed by the Party. They are more concerned with its ideals and symbols than with the acts of the professional party workers and leaders. They vote for the Party ideal rather than for the Party record.

Outside this second ring lies that vast body of people who are not attached to any Party. It is a floating population. The reason for their being unattached is either because they are aimless, thoughtless, or because they have particular interests which are not included in the platform of any Party. Those outside the second ring constitute the most vital field of action for a political Party. They are the prize which a Party must capture. To capture this prize it is not enough to enunciate principles and formulate policies. Men are not interested in principles and policies. But they are interested in accomplishing things. What is necessary for a Party is to bring about concerted action. For in the words of President Woodrow Wilson, given self-government with a majority rule, things can be accomplished not by individual voice but by concerted action.

Now for concerted action, what is necessary is the crystallization of individual opinions into public opinion. This crystallization or building up of public opinion as a sanction behind a particular principle becomes the main function of a Party. Theoretically, political parties are agencies for the expression and execution of public opinion; but in practice, Parties create, direct, influence, and often control public opinion. Indeed this is the chief function of a Party. For this, a Party must do two things. In the first place it must establish contact with the masses. It must go out among the masses with its wares—its principles, policies, ideas, and candidates. In the second place it must carry on propaganda among the masses in favour of its wares. It must animate them and enlighten them, to quote Bryce again "give the voters some knowledge of the political issues they have to decide, to inform them of their leaders, and the crimes of their opponents." These are the basic factors from which concerted action can arise. A Party which fails to forge concerted action has no right to call itself a party.

Which of these things the Liberal Party has done as an organization? The Liberal Party has only the High Command. It has no machine. Not having any machine, the high command is only a shadow. Its following is confined to that second concentric ring consisting of persons who are bound by ties of tradition. The leaders have nothing to evoke emotional loyalty. They have no war cry to gather a crowd. The Liberal Party does not believe in mass contact. It would be difficult to imagine a Party so completely isolated and insulated from the main mass of people. It does not believe in conversion. Not that it has no Gospel to preach; but like the Hindu religion it is a nonproselytising creed. It believes in the formulation of principles and policies. But it does not work for giving effect to them. Propaganda and concerted action are anathema to the Liberal Party. Individual voices and annual meetings, and clamour for invitation when a Cripps arrives or when the Viceroy decides to invite important individuals, have become the limits of its political activity.

Is there any wonder if the Liberal Party has fallen into disrepute? The Liberal Party has forgotten the most elementary fact: that organization is essential for the accomplishment of any purpose and particularly in politics, where the harnessing of so many divergent elements in a working unity is so great.

Who is responsible for this collapse of the Liberal Party in India? However much we may regret to have to say it, I think it will have to be admitted that the responsibility for this catastrophe does to some extent fall on Ranade. Ranade belonged to the [upper] Classes. He was born and bred among them. He never became a man of [the] masses. The Liberal Party has no machine, and the reason why it did not forge a machine is because it did not believe in mass contact. This aversion to mass contact is the legacy of Ranade. In avoiding mass contact the party is following the tradition left by Ranade.

There is another legacy of Ranade to the Liberal Party, and that relates to the false faith in the driving force of principles and policies. Mazzini once said: "You may kill men, you cannot kill a great idea." To me it appears to be a most mistaken view. Men are mortal. So are ideas. It is wrong to hold that an idea will take roots *proprio vigore*. An idea needs propagation as much as a plant needs watering. Both will otherwise wither and die. Ranade agreed with Mazzini and did not believe that the fructification of an idea needed the resources of strenuous husbandry. If the Liberal Party is content with mere formulation of principles and policies, it is also because of this tradition of Ranade.

What is the duty of the Liberals? All Liberals I know will say, our duty is to follow the master. What else could be the attitude of a devout band of disciples? But can anything be more mistaken or more uncritical? Such an attitude implies two things. It means that a great man works by imposing his maxims on his disciples. It means that the disciples should not be wiser than the master. Both these conclusions are wrong. They do injustice to the master. No great man really does his work by crippling his disciple by forcing on them his maxims or his conclusions. What a Great Man does is not to impose his maxims on his disciples. What he does is to evoke them, to awaken them to a vigorous and various exertion of their faculties. Again the pupil only takes his guidance from his master. He is not bound to accept his master's conclusions. There is no ingratitude in the disciple not accepting the maxims or the conclusions of his master. For even when he rejects them he is bound to acknowledge to his master in deep reverence: "You awakened me to be myself; for that I thank you." The master is not entitled to less. The disciple is not bound to give more.

It is therefore [a] wrong to the master as well as to himself, for the disciple to bind himself to the maxims and conclusions of his Master. His duty is to know the principles and, if he is convinced of their value and their worth, to spread them. That is the wish of every Master. Jesus wished it, Buddha wished it. I am sure the same must be the wish of Ranade. It follows that if the Liberals have faith in, and love and respect for, Ranade their supreme duty lies not merely in assembling together to sing his praises, but in organising themselves for spreading the Gospel of Ranade.

What hope is there of the Liberals coming forward to fulfill this duty? Signs are very depressing. In the last election the Liberals did not even contest the seats. That of course is in itself a matter of some surprise. But this pales into nothing when one recalls the announcement made by the Rt. Hon'ble Srinivas Shastri—the Leading Light of the Liberal Party—that he wished the Congress to succeed!! There is no parallel to this except in the treacherous and treasonous conduct of Bhishma, who lived on the bounty of the Kauravas but wished and worked for success to their enemies the Pandavas. This shows even the Liberals had lost faith in the gospel of Ranade. If this is the general condition of health of the Liberal Party, it is [=would be] better if the party died. It would clear the way for a new orientation, and spare us the tedium of idle clatter of liberals and liberalism. For such an event even Ranade may [=might] express satisfaction from his grave.